IN THE
NATIONAL INTEREST

General Sir John Monash once exhorted a graduating class to 'equip yourself for life, not solely for your own benefit but for the benefit of the whole community'. At the university established in his name, we repeat this statement to our own graduating classes, to acknowledge how important it is that common or public good flows from education.

Universities spread and build on the knowledge they acquire through scholarship in many ways, well beyond the transmission of this learning through education. It is a necessary part of a university's role to debate its findings, not only with other researchers and scholars, but also with the broader community in which it resides.

Publishing for the benefit of society is an important part of a university's commitment to free intellectual inquiry. A university provides civil space for such inquiry by its scholars, as well as for investigations by public intellectuals and expert practitioners.

This series, In the National Interest, embodies Monash University's mission to extend knowledge and encourage informed debate about matters of great significance to Australia's future.

Professor Sharon Pickering
President and Vice-Chancellor,
Monash University

KEVIN BELL

HOUSING: THE GREAT AUSTRALIAN RIGHT

MONASH
UNIVERSITY
PUBLISHING

Monash University Publishing
Matheson Library Annexe
40 Exhibition Walk
Monash University
Clayton, Victoria 3800, Australia
https://publishing.monash.edu

Monash University Publishing brings to the world publications which advance the best traditions of humane and enlightened thought.

ISBN: 9781922979759 (paperback)
ISBN: 9781922979773 (ePub)

Series: In the National Interest
Editor: Greg Bain
Project manager & copyeditor: Paul Smitz
Designer: Peter Long
Typesetter: Cannon Typesetting
Proofreader: Gillian Armitage
Printed in Australia by Ligare Book Printers

A catalogue record for this book is available from the National Library of Australia.

The paper this book is printed on is in accordance with the standards of the Forest Stewardship Council. The FSC promotes environmentally responsible, socially beneficial and economically viable management of the world's forests.

HOUSING: THE GREAT AUSTRALIAN RIGHT

Australia is experiencing a housing disaster that no generation should have to live through. There are too few affordable dwellings to buy or rent. In fact, housing affordability in 2024 is the worst on record.[1] Social housing has been run down for decades. Over 120 000 people are living with homelessness. Particularly affected are First People experiencing the continuing impact of colonisation, women with children fleeing domestic violence, people living with mental illness, and low-income older people, especially older women. Across generations, people are anxious about accessing housing, including the young and those on low–middle incomes who face insecure or poor housing for life. Housing anxiety is why the 'Great Australian Dream' is now frequently called the 'Great Australian Nightmare'.

The baby-boomer generation, which includes me, grew up in a very different era. I was born in 1954 to young parents who had eight children. Hundreds of thousands of houses were built by the government that low–middle-income families like ours could afford to rent or buy. We rented a basic three-bedroom weatherboard house from the Victorian Housing Commission in Moorabbin, a south-eastern suburb of Melbourne— fittingly, in the language of the local Bunurong/ Boonwurrung people, 'Moorabbin' means 'resting place' or 'mother's milk'. My maternal grandparents joined us in a bungalow built for a song out the back. As I grew older, it was my job to take the rent to the commission office just down the road. When government policy changed to allow sitting tenants to buy their homes at concessional prices, my parents did so, although they still called the money I took to the same office 'rent'. I owe my family upbringing in a decent home to social housing. However, this is now confined to people in the category of greatest need.

Australia supports the Sustainable Development Goals (SDGs) that were adopted by the General Assembly of the United Nations (UN) in 2015 as an international plan of action to end poverty and to promote peace, prosperity and economically sustainable development. The SDGs 'seek to realise the human rights of all'. SDG 11 is: 'Make cities and human settlements inclusive, safe, resilient and sustainable.' Target 11.1 for that goal is: 'By 2030, ensure access to all to adequate, safe and affordable housing and basic services …'[2] Australia is not on track to meet this target, because of a system failure in which profit has been put before people.

Housing in Australia has become primarily a commodity or investment. Governments have neglected their fundamental obligation to realise everyone's human right to housing and home as the foundation of their personal, social and economic life and participation in society.[3] Governments and policymakers tend not to think about housing in terms of human rights, or they just pay lip-service to this. But human rights are absolutely fundamental and must be taken seriously. This book argues for a shift in the values underpinning the housing system towards recognising a decent home as the 'Great Australian Right'. It argues for making the realisation of this right for everybody the primary purpose of the system and calls for a national housing strategy to bring this about.

A SYSTEM-WIDE PROBLEM

Housing in Australia is a four-part system:

1 home ownership
2 private rental housing
3 social housing
4 homelessness.

All these parts are interconnected in ways that really matter to people over the course of their lives. The current housing disaster demonstrates this. Many households cannot afford and may have to leave home ownership for private rental housing. If they are not able to find an affordable rental, they may need social housing, which is very difficult to obtain, or face homelessness. Many of us are only one personal, work or business emergency away from losing our homes.

Government is responsible for creating a system that fulfils the need for a decent home across the entire cycle of peoples' lives, and for all living generations. But that is not how the system of housing in Australia presently operates. Recent government action and proposed further steps, while welcome, will not be enough. These are directed at ameliorating the problem, not solving it and then ensuring it never happens again.

Home Ownership

Studies show that home ownership is the form of housing most Australians prefer.[4] There are obvious rational and not just psychological reasons for this. But home ownership has become such a dominant focus of the system that it is crowding out consideration of other viable forms of housing, such as rental housing. And it has become very unaffordable. The dream of *universal* access to home ownership in Australia has become a myth, if not an outright lie.

Home ownership is down from a peak of 71 per cent in 1966 to 66 per cent now. And even this aggregate rate of 66 per cent creates a false impression: it is being held up by the relatively unchanged high rate of ownership among older people. Home ownership is plummeting in other age brackets, and especially for younger households and low–middle-income earners of all ages. The share of households aged 25–34 owning their own home fell from 51 per cent in 1997–98 to 41 per cent in 2019–20. For households aged 35–44, the fall was from 70 per cent to 57 per cent, and for those aged 45–54 it dropped from 83 per cent to 72 per cent. Between 1981 and 2016, home ownership rates among those aged 25–34 fell from more than 60 per cent to 45 per cent— for the poorest 40 per cent of that group, the rate has more than halved.

Plummeting home ownership among younger age brackets is happening at the same time as significantly rising housing prices. Low- and even middle-income home buyers are being priced out of the market. House prices rose by an extraordinary 42 per cent and units by 19.3 per cent between early 2020 and early 2024. Between January 2023 and March 2024, house prices rose 10.5 per cent and unit prices by 7.8 per cent. Nationally, the share of homes that a medium-income household can afford to buy fell from 39 per cent in 2020–21 to 13 per cent in 2022–23, the lowest level on record.

In an article in *Quarterly Essay*, Alan Kohler tells the housing story of three generations of his own family, highlighting the importance of the average wage/housing price ratio. His parents bought land on which they built a house in the 1950s, paying about 3.5 times the average wage (his father was the one person earning near that wage). Alan and his wife bought their first house in 1980, also paying about 3.5 times the average wage (two wage earners on that wage). Their three children bought houses in the 2020s, paying 7.5 times the average wage (also two wage earners but on more than that wage).

As Kohler explains, until about 2000, average wages and house prices were rising at about the same rate, so the wage/price ratio for buying a house remained at about 3.5. After 2000, the price of houses rose markedly but average earnings did not. By August 2023, the wage/price ratio was 7.4 for the median Australian house price of $732 886.[5]

A great many Australian families will see themselves in this story. Young adults today have to pay for a home with more than twice as much of their income as their parents and grandparents did—if they can. So much for the idea that if you get a good education and job and work hard, you can always buy a house in this country. Then there is the record high deposit hurdle. Aspiring homeowners have to save for over ten years for a 20 per cent deposit. Hundreds of thousands of us cannot, and not everyone can call on the 'bank of mum and dad'. This situation is increasing income and wealth inequality both across and between generations, and decreasing social participation and inclusion.

According to the Productivity Commission,

[t]he bottom line is that Australia's home ownership rate is falling. By age, falling ownership rates are most pronounced in younger households. Households are buying their first home later in life. And at all ages, each successive birth cohort generally has lower ownership rates than cohorts that came before them. By income, the biggest falls in home ownership are by households around the middle of the income distribution.[6]

This is indeed a disastrous state of affairs. Too many of a whole generation of ordinary working people and their families cannot expect to own their own home. It comes down to basic personal and family economics, and the arithmetic is not difficult. Housing prices have risen so high that most people on low–medium wages wanting to buy a house or a two-bedroom apartment simply cannot. Even if there are two income earners in the household, they would have to wait too long to save for the deposit and their income would be too low to meet the high mortgage payments. And this even with historically low interest rates. There is no way this situation is consistent with our federal government's accepted obligation to give effect to everyone's human right to a decent home.

Some people, as their incomes rise with better-paid jobs and they manage to save a deposit, will be able to afford buying a home or apartment, especially if they receive parental help. This is the main reason why, on average, people are buying homes and having children later in life. In the meantime, they may have to obtain a private rental, as will people who cannot afford ever to buy a home and are not eligible for social housing. Unfortunately, the situation concerning the private rental housing part of the system is also disastrous.

Private Rental Housing

Housing stress is a serious national problem. It is a situation in which households in the bottom 40 per cent of the income distribution have to pay more than 30 per cent of their income to meet their 'housing cost burden' (the '30/40' rule).[7]

It is now usual for low-income tenants to experience housing stress, many severely so, and this is only increasing. In 2019–20, 42 per cent of low-income renters (more than 600 000 Australian households) experienced rental stress, up from 35 per cent in 2007–08. Two-thirds of low-income private renters spent over 30 per cent of their income on rent in 2019–20, while 20 per cent spent half of their income on rent.[8] This housing stress is adding to poverty and inequality. In relative terms, over the past twenty-five years, low-income renters have been less able to meet rising housing costs than higher-income renters. About 22 per cent of low-income, privately renting households have less than $250 left each week after paying rent—in other words, they are living in poverty and are at extreme risk of homelessness. It is staggering to think that nearly half of all retirees live in poverty.[9] We owe them better. Respecting their human rights demands better.

This is occurring because private rents have risen markedly over time, especially in recent years, and vacancy rates are very low and falling. In April 2024, the national vacancy rate was 1 per cent and capital city average rents had increased 10.2 per cent for the year.[10] There are very few affordable houses for rental. In some areas, there is virtually no rental housing for low-income earners. In recent times, low-income private renters have confronted an ever-growing national deficit of private rentals, one that swelled from 48 000 to an astonishing 212 000 in the two decades to 2016.[11]

Caitlin's experience is not uncommon. She was working in the homelessness sector in Perth when she almost became homeless herself due to steep rental increases. The 33-year-old was living in a dual-income household in the city's inner east, caring for her fifteen-year-old child who has severe autism, when the problems started to snowball. From October 2023, Caitlin and her partner experienced housing stress, falling behind on rent and facing eviction notices. She worked in a position where she was supposed to be helping people but became someone who had to reach out for help; she carried a lot of shame about that. In December 2023, she and her family were about to be forced onto the streets when they were saved by the state government's rent relief scheme. This allows tenants in private rentals to access a one-off support payment up to $5000 to cover rental arrears. Caitlin was able to pay off the backload of rent and get back on her feet. Without this assistance, she would have had to split up her family and live in a share house.[12]

Caitlin's household is among the 26 per cent of Australian households living in a private rental, making them a 'key component of the housing spectrum'.[13] This is a substantial proportion of the Australian population. And the percentage has been increasing at the expense of both owner-occupation and social housing for decades.

Commonwealth rent assistance (CRA) is an income supplement for about 1.35 million households renting privately or from community housing providers, and who fall within certain income support categories. Its cost had reached $5.3 billion a year by 2022. However, as at June 2022, 63 per cent of CRA recipients were paying more than 30 per cent of their income on rent (housing stress) and 23 per cent paid more than half their income on rent (severe housing stress); 79 per cent received

CRA at the maximum rate, so it cannot rise in the event of further rent increases. The supplement did go up by 15 per cent in the 2023–24 federal Budget and a further 10 per cent in the 2024–25 Budget, but while a welcome amelioration, this is no solution, because the problem is an order of magnitude larger.

It is unsurprising that, as the home ownership sector of the housing system has become unaffordable, private renting has been growing, a pattern that is likely to continue. This is but one obvious example of how the four parts of the housing system interact. More people are now long-term renters. In 2015, 56 per cent of people had been renting for five years, up from 46 per cent in 2001. But a longer period of renting is not necessarily evidence of secure renting because it does not usually involve a single dwelling. Two-thirds of renters move within two years, as against one-quarter of owners with a mortgage.[14] Many are forced to move, which is highly disruptive, especially for households with children.

Another example of how different parts of the housing system interact is that the need for social housing increases when the availability of affordable private rental housing decreases. Therefore, when calculating the 'right' level of social housing, the Productivity Commission takes into account systemic factors. These include how well private rental markets work for people on low incomes or those experiencing vulnerability, and the existing level of demand for social and affordable housing in the relevant community.[15] But it is not only the lack of affordable private rental housing that increases the need for social housing. This also occurs when the private rental housing that is available and affordable is not safe and secure, which is a function of weak residential tenancy laws.

Tenancy regulation has a very light touch in Australia, often failing to adequately protect tenants' human rights. As the Patron of Tenants Victoria, which was formed nearly fifty years ago to promote and protect the rights of renters in the state, I am especially concerned about this. Even though renting is the only housing choice for many, it is seen to be a second-best choice and so it gets second-best legal protection. It says a lot about what Australian lawmakers value that tenancy laws better protect the property rights of investor-owners than they do the human rights of their renters.

Tenancy laws have never been in balance in this country, yet the human right to a decent home requires that they be in balance. Where is the dignity in living with insecurity of tenure, excessive rent increases and even substandard housing? This decreases confidence in private rental housing as an appealing and appropriate alternative to social housing, especially for long-term occupation. If private rental housing were more available and affordable, and safer and more secure, more people would choose it, as they do in other countries that have balanced tenancy laws that respect human rights.

Social Housing

Social housing includes both public rental housing that is owned and managed directly by state or territory governments, including for Indigenous people, and community rental housing—including Indigenous community housing—which is owned or managed by community organisations, mostly not for profit. Public rental housing comprises about 75 per cent of social housing, a number that is falling; community rental housing is about 25 per cent and rising.

Social housing has been in significant decline in Australia, which is a major contributor to the housing disaster. It is down to a residual model where eligibility is confined to people living on pensions and benefits in circumstances of greatest need.[16]

Natalia grew up in foster homes and then lived on the street. She started living with a man who did nothing but beat her. One day she collapsed and was rushed to hospital, where doctors said they weren't expecting her to live. But she did. She remembers praying and fighting like mad, hanging onto the bars of the bed, saying 'You're not taking me, you're not taking me.' The doctors told her they didn't want her to go back to her partner. The Office of Housing was contacted and it offered her a house. She moved in with one sheet—that's all she had—and slept on the floor. But bit by bit, she built herself up, to the point that she described never having been happier in her life. She made her home very comfortable, with a beautiful garden. Having a home gave her a chance to start living again—she said she now felt like a butterfly.[17]

In 2021, some 418 000 households—790 000 people— were living like Natalia in social housing, which was 4.2 per cent of all households, down from 4.7 per cent in 2008 and the all-time high of 6 per cent in 1991. Most live in public housing as tenants—some 288 345 households (about 70 per cent) in 2021. But the community rental housing sector is large and growing, amounting to 108 500 dwellings in 2021, triple the figure in 2006.

Australian social housing chronically falls well short of meeting people's needs. Governments have kept the sector down to one-third behind population growth for decades.[18] The stock in 2022 was about 443 000 dwellings, up only slightly from 428 000 in 2013; of the 176 000 people applying for social housing in 2021, over 40 per cent were in the greatest need category. Waiting lists are long and have been rising since 2018, increasing at an annual rate of 3.8 per cent in the five years to 2022–23 when they reached 169 000 people. The number of greatest need and First People households rose much faster, at 8.7 per cent and 10 per cent respectively. Instead of maintaining or growing the direct provision of public rental housing, governments have shifted public funding to the provision of rental assistance payments, to enable households to access the private market, where they typically experience rental housing stress.

Housing unaffordability and the experience of homelessness are linked.[19] Unaffordable rents, low vacancy rates, and poor-quality, insecure private rental housing increase the need for social housing. Where this is not available when needed, or at all, the experience of homelessness can be the result. Indeed, it is now the reality for significant numbers of people, which is a national disgrace.

Homelessness

To experience homelessness is not just to be roofless or live on the streets. This is acknowledged in the definition of 'homelessness' offered by the Australian Bureau of Statistics, which is widely accepted. It joins up the physical idea of a house with the social idea of a home.[20] Drawing on human rights, it captures what people need in a home to live a dignified life: security, stability, privacy, safety, and being able to control one's living space. By this definition, a person experiences homelessness if, having no other alternative, they are living in an inadequate dwelling, their dwelling has no tenure or it is short and not extendable, or they do not have control of, or access to, space for social relations.

Using this definition, we see that homelessness is rising in Australia, fuelled by housing unaffordability and long social housing waiting lists. On Census night in 2021, 122 494 people experienced homelessness, up by over 6000 from 2016. The number of people experiencing homelessness was 45.2 per 10 000 in 2006, 50 per 10 000 in 2016 and 48 per 10 000 in 2021—the small decline in 2021 was due to COVID measures, which proves what can be done when the political will exists. Of those homeless, 17 646 (14.4 per cent) were aged under twelve years, 25 504 (20.8 per cent) were aged 25–34, and 17 085 (13.9 per cent) were aged 35–44. In fact, homelessness among those aged eighteen and under is increasing,[21] and homelessness in Australia remained among the highest in Organisation for Economic Co-operation and Development countries in 2021.

The number of Aboriginal and Torres Strait Islander people living in homelessness is very high and also rising, numbering 29 930 in 2021—up 6.4 per cent from 2016. This amounts to one in five (20.4 per cent) of all people experiencing homelessness in Australia. As Aboriginal and Torres Strait Islander people constitute 3.2 per cent of the Australian population, this further means they are six times more likely to be living in homelessness. In 2021, 307 Aboriginal and Torres Strait Island persons per 10 000 people were experiencing homelessness, six times the national rate of forty-eight persons per 10 000.[22]

Contrary to the popular perception, homelessness is not a problem that exists only on the fringes of Australian life. In 2019, some 2.2 million people in Australia had been without a permanent place to live at some point in their lives.[23]

Grace's story is not unusual. She was in her late forties, had five children and was a victim/survivor of family violence when she separated from her husband in Melbourne. She initially rented with all her children, but being reliant on income support payments, Grace and her children often had to choose between food and paying the rent. In 2021, Grace was able to secure another rented home from her real estate agent. This property included a defective toilet and other substandard features which precipitated two of her older teenage children leaving the house to live with family friends. She subsequently could not afford to pay the rent on this home because she was not regularly working. She was evicted again and, as she could not obtain social housing, the family became homeless. They began couch surfing as they searched for another home.[24]

At the level of an individual like Grace, many factors may contribute to homelessness. These include poverty, mental ill-health, relationship breakdown, rental housing stress, violence against women and, for First People, discrimination. However, even then, homelessness should not be inevitable.

A person does not have to earn their human right to a decent home by avoiding the adverse vicissitudes of life. Persons always have, and can never lose, the human right to a decent home, including emergency or short-term accommodation when needed. Homelessness occurs when governments fail to ensure everyone has access to that home or accommodation, whatever the circumstances. Homelessness is evidence of a national policy failure because it is caused by structural factors that lead to housing unaffordability, over which government has control.[25] It is a failure for which government is responsible.

In the words of Leilani Fahra, who was the UN special rapporteur on the right to adequate housing from 2014 until 2020: 'Homelessness is a profound assault on dignity, social inclusion and the right to life. It is a prima facie violation of the right to housing and violates a number of other human rights …'[26]

A HUMAN RIGHTS PERSPECTIVE

Colonial Origins

The housing disaster is not a random natural event like an earthquake or a tsunami, although its effects are as great or greater. What kind of housing society gets is a matter of democratic choice, and whether all members of society can equally access decent housing depends upon that choice. The housing disaster is a direct result of government policy formulated and implemented in the name of the people over a long period of time. It is occurring because government has pushed housing valued as a commodity for producing private wealth ahead of housing valued as a home. It has put profit ahead of people. This is the opposite of valuing a decent home as a human right. In Australia, the origin of the idea that housing is to be valued primarily as a commodity for producing private wealth is colonisation. It is part of our creation story. We need to recognise this and start thinking differently.

The traditional owners of the Mornington Peninsula in what is now known as Victoria are the Bunurong/Boonwurrung people of the Kulin nation, who have never ceded sovereignty. 'Balnarring', which names Country on the Western Port Bay side of the peninsula, comes from the Kulin word for 'camp', a home-place of greater or lesser duration. It is my home-place, in which I wrote this book. Nearby is a place called Sandy Point, where, in 1836, a ship arrived carrying Joseph Tice Gellibrand, one of many settlers who came to take land from traditional owners in the earliest days of Victorian colonisation.

Gellibrand disembarked with hundreds of sheep and headed north-west towards Port Phillip Bay (known to Indigenous people as Narrm). It was January, the height of summer, and the party became hot and thirsty.

They were close to death when they found water near 'about a hundred native huts' not far from Balnarring, and many 'native wells' elsewhere.[27] I have observed the beautiful and sheltered place where this settlement was located, within the wide elbow of a creek. Early European maps show open plains nearby, doubtless produced by firestick farming, where hunting could take place. The existence of so many huts gives the lie to the common myth that First People did not have physical settlements. But that is not my point. I want to contrast Gellibrand's idea of land with that of the traditional owners.

The Bunurong/Boonwurrung count among other First People as the oldest continuous human cultures on earth. Their land was (is, and always will be) the spiritual foundation of their collective existence. It was their home in the fullest sense of that word. Under their culture, the land was respected and nurtured as a vital life force. First People today call this 'caring for Country'. A hundred huts suggest 200-plus people lived in the vicinity. There likely would have been important ceremonial and burial places nearby. This human settlement was underpinned by a system of traditional land law which extended to how the huts were arranged in that space and how they interacted with the surrounding area. Owned by and for the whole community, the land was sustainably utilised for hunting, gathering, medicine, mining, trading, and in many other productive ways. The community had an economy and understood notions of wealth and value, but this was not the primary purpose of land, which was seen holistically. It was part of a system in balance. Homelessness did not exist.[28]

We can infer from his conduct that Gellibrand had a completely different idea about land. For him, it was property from which wealth could be derived. Ignoring the prior rights of the traditional owners, he saw land purely as a physical resource to be claimed and used for his enrichment—an instrument of maximum private gain. He thought nothing of coming onto the Country of the Bunurong/Boonwurrung and running sheep there without permission for as long as he wished. This land was a physical object he could exclusively own once the often-violent dispossession was legally mandated in the colonisers' law, and then it could be kept or sold for private gain, as he saw fit. The land might become Gellibrand's home, but that was not its primary purpose. He could stay, move on, or take (or buy) other land if he wished, which in fact he did. Like other settlers, he behaved according to the 'central colonial mode—to extract wealth from land'.[29]

This dichotomy between how settlers and traditional owners saw land is between land valued primarily as a commodity for producing private wealth, and land valued in a holistic way, including as a home-place.

As others writing about housing in Australia have observed, the exploitation of land valued primarily as a commodity and an instrument of private gain is a colonial idea.[30] Settlers brought this idea with them and ensured that it stayed. In fact, promoting and acting on this idea was the main purpose of colonisation. The same dichotomy is playing out in the modern age.

First People are the most affected by today's housing disaster. They were dispossessed of their land and home-places at colonisation. When this happened, gross human rights violations were perpetrated upon them, including massacres. Despite this, First People have maintained their deep cultural connection with, and knowledge of, land and how it can be sustainably managed, used and shared—productively, culturally and otherwise. Yet they are the least likely to be homeowners, and the most likely to be tenants, have the greatest numbers living in social housing and have greater experience of homelessness than any other segment of the population. Through their resilience and advocacy, a mix of voice, truth and treaty processes have been established in some states to address these historic and ongoing injustices—and there is much to be reckoned with.[31] Recognising and implementing the right of First People to self-determination in respect of their land, housing and culture is fundamental both to the success of these processes and to addressing the housing disaster as it relates to Indigenous Australians.[32]

The Postwar Period

In the period immediately following World War II, the balance between land valued as a commodity and land valued as a home was struck differently. After two world wars and the Depression, the national housing stock was poor in quality and there was a shortage of housing for the general population, especially with thousands of service personnel due to return from overseas. Social housing expenditure was seen as necessary infrastructure investment in support of postwar social and economic reconstruction.

Consequently, in 1943, the minister of state for postwar construction in the Curtin Labor government, Ben Chifley, established a Commonwealth Housing Commission (CHC) under wartime national security regulations. Its terms of reference were to inquire into and report upon '(a) The present housing position in Australia; and (b) The housing requirements of Australia during the post-war period'. In its report, the commission stated its fundamental philosophical position: 'a *dwelling of good standard and equipment is not only the need but the right of every citizen*—whether the dwelling is to be rented or purchased, no tenant or purchaser should be exploited for excessive profit'.[33]

As this statement makes clear, the commission was not anti–home ownership as a form of tenure, and it assumed the continuation of the private market. But it was primarily concerned with ensuring that everyone had access to decent housing, especially the low-income group. This was the gap to be filled to obtain a balanced housing system operating inclusively for all. Expanding rental housing as a good form of tenure to stand alongside home ownership was the best filler of that gap. This message still has resonance today.

The commission's report emphasised the significance of national housing planning. If it had come to pass, this would have been Australia's first and only national housing plan, one based on universal human rights, and Australian housing would have developed differently. Unfortunately, the pertinent recommendations were not implemented due to opposition from the states. Nonetheless, the linchpin of the report was a recommendation for establishing a national rental housing program for people who could not or would not buy a house privately, to be funded by the Commonwealth and administered by the states. This was implemented as the historic Commonwealth State Housing Agreement (CSHA), which was legislated in 1945,[34] and renewed many times thereafter in the postwar period.

Historians of the CSHA record that the construction of new public rental housing rose significantly under the first agreement as a result of direct government investment.[35] Eligibility for this housing was deliberately set at above safety net levels to include low–middle-income earning households. Rents were set at levels that were affordable to those households. So as to ensure the level of stock would be maintained, sitting tenants were not permitted to buy the dwellings. The agreement made a major contribution to realising the right to a decent home for all.

The Liberal–Country Party Coalition came to power in 1949. In a campaign speech in Melbourne on 10 November, Robert Menzies committed his government to amending the CSHA 'so as to permit and aid "little Capitalists" to own their own homes'. As Menzies' biographer has argued, this policy was never just about wealth accumulation and individual gain (although its modern version is much more so). It was also about nation-building—'building a stable society and a functioning democracy' based on the domestic, social and economic value of housing.[36]

Amend the CSHA the Menzies government did. The new policy was to grow private capital in the form of home ownership, but it was *not* economically laissez-faire. From being a vehicle for increasing public rental housing, the CSHA was transformed into a vehicle for direct government investment in private home ownership. Hundreds of thousands of dwellings were constructed under the CSHA in the following decades, which ended up in private hands. Home ownership increased and public rental housing decreased. Dwellings were sold to sitting tenants. Commonwealth housing funding was diverted to a housing purchase program for middle-income earners—Menzies' 'Forgotten People', from the title of his famous 1942 radio broadcast. By these and other means, home ownership reached a peak of 71.4 per cent in 1966 that has never been exceeded. In the words of Peter Mares, Menzies set Australia 'on a path that turned housing into real estate and transformed its primary role from meeting a fundamental human need to serving as an asset class'.[37]

However, even this level of direct government investment in the housing system was not enough fully to meet the needs of the population. It was just a much better effort than had previously been made. Nor was this effort maintained when direct government investment in housing (or in practically anything) became increasingly unpopular in the later neoliberal age. From the mid-1950s to the mid-1970s, public sector agencies built an average of 15 512 new dwellings per year. From the mid-1970s to the early-1990s, this dropped to 12 379 per year. The average then fell to 6000 per year by 2013, with a nadir of less than 4000 per year between 1999 and 2009. Social housing as a percentage of housing stock peaked in 1991 at 5.6 per cent and fell fully one-third to 3.8 per cent in 2021.

As a consequence, public rental housing became what it is today—a residual part of the housing system for those in greatest need that is chronically underdeveloped. Social housing is so short in supply that waiting lists are in the tens of thousands, waiting times are in the tens of years, and both are climbing. The shortfall of social housing dwellings is well over 500 000, and may indeed be closer to 1 000 000. Homelessness support services are in a constant state of crisis. If this trajectory continues, the long-term outlook is terrifying.

The Contemporary Scene

The contemporary scene in Australia, by which I mean post-2000, reflects the market-based housing system that has been in place since colonisation. Depending upon the degree of government intervention in that market, the balance between land valued as a commodity and land valued as a home has varied over time. But for the past few decades, the commodity focus has dominated. In the housing system now, home ownership is privileged, and the role of renting and social housing is diminished; the role of the private sector is paramount and that of the public sector is residual. Today, some 96 per cent of housing (the paramount home ownership and private rental housing sectors) is supplied by and traded in the private market. The remainder (the residual social housing sector) is supplied and allocated by government and by public and community agencies. The private market is underpinned by laws that guarantee strong property rights for owners. Tenancy laws? The opposite.

Housing has reached the point where it is Australia's largest asset class. In 2022, it had a value of $9.615 trillion—four times the capitalised value of the Australian share market. Land and dwellings account for more than half (55 per cent) of the total value of assets held by Australian households. Those households owe a total of $1.4 trillion in loans (landlords owe $640 billion), the highest level of home-ownership debt in the world. A large and politically influential cohort of voting Australians has a huge stake in home ownership and small-scale investment in rental housing as supported by present legal and taxation arrangements.

Home ownership, meanwhile, is unaffordable to households even with two earners on the average wage, rents are skyrocketing, vacancy rates are plummeting, tenancy laws are second-best, social housing is a residual part of the system under chronic strain, and over 120 000 people live in homelessness among the national plenty.

At a high level of generality, it is accepted that these significant affordable and social housing problems are occurring because housing demand is increasing at a time when housing supply is grossly deficient. There are legacy causes, as we just discussed, and others that are complex, multifaceted, and extend across many policy areas and aspects of government.

A big step in growing Australia's institutional capacity to understand these causes was taken by the establishment of the National Housing Supply and

Affordability Council (NHSAC) in 2023. In its first *State of the Housing System* report in 2024, the council addresses the causes in terms of supply and demand, the human consequences and the legacy of the past.[38] The foreword, by council chair Susan Lloyd-Hurwitz, states that the unhealthy Australian housing market 'is not an abstract and theoretical topic. We're talking about homes, not assets. Access to shelter is a basic human need and right.' This picks up strongly where the CHC left off sixty years earlier. The report—as did the CHC— also stresses the need to treat social and affordable housing as 'essential infrastructure'.

Other recent expert writings on the problems confronting the housing system, such as those of Kohler, Brendan Coates from the Grattan Institute, independent economist Saul Eslake, the Productivity Commission, and Chris Martin and his colleagues at the Australian Housing and Urban Research Institute (AHURI),[39] are broadly consistent with the report and each other. A good basis now exists for understanding the contemporary causes of the housing disaster, to which, in this book, I wish to contribute a human rights perspective.

In Australia, housing supply is relatively inelastic. It does not respond sufficiently to demand. There are many reasons for this, including the cost and availability of labour, materials and equipment; difficulties in accessing project finance; the availability of land; and (some say) slow and costly development processes; all on top of the legacy of social and affordable housing shortages. Not enough housing—and especially *that* kind of housing—has been built directly by government or the private sector.

At the same time, Australia has experienced high and sustained demand for housing. Again, many reasons apply, including population growth; historically high migration unlinked to housing supply; household size reductions leading to household number increases; increasing household incomes (well below increases in housing prices); increasing household wealth (though not equally among all social groups); interest rate reductions; and government policy choices, like tax breaks for investors in housing and first home-buyer grants. Too little of the available housing is affordable and social, or going to those who need to own or rent it most.

In relation to the demand causes of the housing disaster, it is worth recalling Kohler's *Quarterly Review* essay, in which he argues that four things came together around 2000 to greatly fuel investor demand for the supply of housing, and which had profound implications for the nation. He begins with when the Howard government cut capital gains tax to 50 per cent in 1999. Combined with negative gearing (already in place), this greatly increased speculative investment in housing (including existing housing), which was the explicit intention of the policy. This was a full step beyond what the Menzies government intended, which was to encourage home ownership, not landlordism. The value pendulum of the housing system thus swung far in the direction of housing as a commodity and instrument of private gain rather than as a home and human right, and there it will remain until different choices are made.

The consequences of what occurred around 2000 have indeed been disastrous. Investors immediately gained a competitive advantage over home buyers in the housing market. Kohler also points to the resumption of the first home-buyer grant program that year, which increased the price but not the availability or affordability of housing for home ownership. The Reserve Bank of Australia cut interest rates to record low levels in the early 2000s. Lastly, between 2003 and 2009, net migration tripled but was not matched by the supply of new houses. Consequently, Kohler contends:

> The houses we live in, the places we call home and bring up our families in, have been turned into speculative investment assets by the fifty years of government policy failure, financialisation and greed that resulted in twenty-five years of exploding house prices.[40]

National Cabinet, state and territory governments, and the Commonwealth Government have recently adopted a range of measures designed to increase the availability of social and affordable housing, and to improve renters' rights. At the Commonwealth level, these include the formulation of a National Housing and

Homelessness Plan (underway), the National Housing and Homelessness Agreement (2018), the National Housing Accord (2023), the Housing Australia Future Fund (2023), the Social Housing Accelerator (2023), tax measures to support institutional investment in build-to-rent accommodation, and A Better Deal for Renters. These programs are mainly aimed at increasing supply, which government considers to be the fundamental problem. For example, the National Housing Accord is an intergovernmental agreement on a new national target of building 1.2 million affordable homes over five years from mid-2024. The Housing Australia Future Fund is a $10 billion fund to help build 30 000 new social and affordable homes in the first five years, targeted at those with acute housing needs.

These are very welcome steps that shift the balance in the system back towards valuing housing for its role in providing decent homes for people. However, there is a real question mark here over the sufficiency of these measures. The operation of the Australian housing market is grossly deficient. Affordability pressures are high. Social and affordable housing, and housing for the homeless, is way short of what's needed and on a terrifying long-term trajectory. The housing disaster should not simply be ameliorated. It needs to be ended in favour of a system whose purpose is to realise the human right to decent housing for all. This requires long-term thinking beyond the electoral cycles.

One important way of assessing the sufficiency of the measures is to examine their impact on the 'outlook' of the housing system—what will the system look like in a given period if the measures are implemented? In that period, will the measures ensure there is sufficient supply to meet the expected demand for housing, as well as the needs that have built up through previous neglect?

There are two different ways of examining housing outlook: assessments based on the balance between the expected supply of, and demand for, housing over the forecast period; and assessments based on the balance between the expected supply of, and need for, housing over that period. The first method estimates expected net new supply as against expected net new demand arising from net new household formation. It does not take into account existing needs arising from social and affordable housing shortages and homelessness. The second method calculates the need for social and affordable housing and for housing for people living with homelessness, which includes built-up need arising from legacy causes.

The NHSAC went into these matters in detail. It examined the recent initiatives under the first method, which was all that its current model allowed. The forecast period was six financial years, from 2023–24 to 2028–29. It found that, even including the 1.2 million new affordable homes in the National Housing Accord, there would be a significant shortfall of new supply relative to new demand, of around 37 000 dwellings in 2023–24 and around 39 000 dwellings over that six-year period. The council's conclusion pulled no punches:

> These shortfalls in new supply relative to new demand will add to the already significant undersupply of housing in the system in the absence of a significant change in housing policy or the capacity of the housing sector to supply new dwellings … As a result, housing affordability is expected to deteriorate further over the forecast horizon.

The NHSAC accepted that its model did 'not reflect the significant unmet need and affordability pressures that have already accumulated in the housing system', including the unmet need relating to homelessness. But it accepted that this need existed. Again, it pulled no punches: 'There will be no surplus of new housing supply to address the significant unmet need for housing that currently exists due to affordability constraints, or to accommodate the 122 000 Australians experiencing homelessness …'[41]

Calculating housing need is a very important matter for those committed to ensuring everyone has access to a decent home; that is, ensuring the human right to that home is realised. It is an essential planning tool. Unfortunately, at present, calculating housing need is an inexact and evolving field of scholarship. I hope it receives more attention. But there are reliable studies that support the conclusion of the NHSAC.

The National Housing Finance and Investment Corporation, in its *State of the Nation's Housing 2022–23* report, conservatively estimated that, in the year in question, 46 500 dwellings were needed to house the homeless population and 331 100 households needed social and affordable housing: a total of 377 600 households in need of housing. It said that housing need across the country ranged from 208 200 to 577 400 households, depending on the measure of rental stress used in estimating the need.[42]

The Productivity Commission report *In Need of Repair* refers to three studies. The first, undertaken in 2019, calculated that in the twenty years from 2016, Australia would require 727 400 social housing dwellings—433 400 of them for people experiencing homelessness and for the poorest households in housing stress, at a cost of around $10 billion a year (a total of $200 billion). The second study, also from 2019, yielded similar results, estimating an additional need over twenty years of 728 600 social housing dwellings at a cost of between $4 billion and $5 billion a year (a total of $80 billion to $100 billion). The third study, from 2021, found that the cost of building an additional 727 400 dwellings as recommended in the first study would be $290 billion, not $200 billion, over twenty years.[43]

A further study was based on 2021 Census data. It found that an additional 942 000 social and affordable housing dwellings would be needed to meet current unmet and future needs projected over twenty years to 2041. This implies a sustained annual growth rate of 6.5 per cent, or a net 47 000 extra dwellings, per year. Costings were not included in this study.[44]

Whichever method of assessing government initiatives is adopted, a yawning gap appears between what is needed and what has been announced. The housing disaster, with its deep and longstanding causes, is not going away. A new way of thinking must be adopted, one that applies human rights to understanding the problem, and ultimately ensures that the realisation of the human right to a decent home is a central part of the solution.

REFRAMING THE HOUSING DISASTER

Housing as a Pillar of the Human Rights System

The housing disaster in Australia is not only a socio-economic disaster. It is also a human rights disaster. Decent housing is a pillar of the whole human rights system. When the right to a decent home is put at risk or violated on a large scale, this impacts on a great many other rights. These other rights potentially include the right to life; the right to health, including mental health; the right to personal inviolability, including the right of women to be free of violence in their own homes; the right to be free of gender, race, age and other kinds of discrimination; the right to work; the right to education; and the right to be free of human rights violations that are associated with poverty, inequality and homelessness.

Each of these rights is put at risk when people do not have access to a decent home, including emergency or temporary housing when needed; when people must pay well above their means for their housing; or when they have insecure or poor-quality housing, or housing that is unsafe or too distant from family, work, and medical and other necessary services. The risk is so grave when people experience homelessness that this is a prima facie violation of human rights in and of itself.

Many people go into medical or similar care or custodial settings for reasons associated with poor housing or homelessness, and they are discharged from these settings into the same precarious situation. This creates a cycle of entrenched poverty with poor health outcomes, especially for mental health, and a much higher risk of recidivism for people leaving prison. The common cause is a systemic lack of decent housing, especially for people with complex needs.

Human rights laws and principles have evolved to expose what is at stake for individuals when their human rights generally are put at risk by the violation of one right, such as the right to housing. They shed light on the broader human rights implications of the housing disaster.

The starting point is that human rights are universal, indivisible, interdependent and interrelated. This means all human rights belong equally to each person in full and as a system. No person is an island, and neither is any human right. As people strive to realise their inherent potential personally, socially, culturally and economically, so human rights operate as a system to support in law that beautiful endeavour in all its possible dimensions.

Next, people may experience multiple human rights violations at the same time. A person living in housing with faulty wiring is at risk of violation of both the right to safe housing and the right to life—human rights articulate the interests of the person from both points of view.

Finally, some people and groups experience a common kind of stigma or discrimination and may have their rights put at risk in intersecting and compounding ways.[45] In relation to housing, older women generally may (and do) experience both sex and age discrimination, while older Indigenous women may (and do) experience that, plus race discrimination. The different aspects of the rights-violating situation must be addressed singly and collectively. This is a different exercise to just focusing on one aspect.

Housing and the Right to Life

In human rights law, the right to adequate housing is an aspect of the right to an adequate standard of living. The right to be free of unlawful and arbitrary interference with the home is an aspect of the right to have and develop a private (civil) life. These two elements form a kind of compound right guaranteeing housing as a physical place where people can make a home to live and develop without interference as they personally choose.

This human right to a decent home expresses a fundamental human need as a universal legal right that government is obliged to observe. The purpose of the right is to enable people, individually and collectively, to live in security, peace and dignity, and to flourish and participate in society in ways that they choose. Unless people have decent housing, their capacity to do so is limited or nil.

The right to life is a right to be free of arbitrary or unlawful deprivation of life. It is not a right to mere existence but a right to live in dignity. It is not violated only by deliberate, unlawful and unjustified steps taken to kill a person, but also when government fails to take steps to ensure that people can live in dignity. One of the steps that must be taken is to establish a system where everyone can access decent housing, without which it is practically impossible to live in dignity.

It can be seen that the right to a decent home and the right to life protect the same underlying values and interests: enabling all persons to live with dignity and achieve their full potential as they personally choose. This is one reason why the housing disaster is a human rights disaster. Where a person's right to a decent home is endangered, their capacity to live with dignity and achieve their full potential may be endangered, and so may their life.

The point is especially salient in relation to people living with homelessness, who have mortality rates 2–5 times higher than the general population,[46] and who die aged about fifty (some thirty years younger than the general population).[47] These rates are so disproportionately high that I support calls for the mandatory reporting of deaths of people in homelessness to state and territory coroners, who can then investigate the circumstances and make recommendations for reform.

The UN oversight authority for the right to housing is the Committee on Economic, Social and Cultural Rights (CESCR). It has drawn attention to the importance of the relationship between the right to housing and the right to life. In a specific report on this relationship, Leilani Fahra has stated: 'The right to life cannot be separated from the right to a secure place to live, and the right to a secure place to live has meaning only in the context of a right to live in dignity and security, free of violence.'[48]

The UN oversight authority for the right to life is the Human Rights Committee, which has also drawn attention to the relationship between the right to life and the right to housing.[49] This connection was shockingly demonstrated by the Kew Cottages fire in Melbourne in 1996, in which nine intellectually disabled adult men died.[50] I appeared on behalf of the fire brigade during the eight-week inquest, in which the coroner found that a locked ward, no sprinkler system and inadequate fire alarms were to blame for the tragedy. The Victorian Government had met its obligation to ensure the men had housing commensurate with their intellectual disability, but the housing was not safe, which led to their deaths.

Housing and the Right to Health

Large numbers of people in Australia lack adequate mental health and wellbeing. This is a major issue which has been the subject of many official inquiries. The personal, social and economic cost is astronomical. Addressing this issue is a contemporary public policy and also a human rights issue of fundamental importance.

The right to health means the right to enjoyment of the highest attainable standard of physical and mental health. CESCR is also the oversight authority for the right to health. It has stated that this right 'is closely related to and dependent upon the realisation of other human rights', including the right to housing.[51] Nowhere is this more apparent than in relation to mental health, for which a decent home is crucial.

This is another reason why the housing disaster is a human rights disaster. Unaffordable housing, scarce social housing and homelessness on the scale being experienced in Australia are driving extremely poor physical and mental health and other outcomes, for a large segment of the population. Certain population groups are more susceptible to these poor outcomes, including First People, women and children experiencing and fleeing violence in their homes, the LGBTIQ+ population, adults aged fifty-five years and older, young people leaving out-of-home care, and people leaving institutions like prisons. This is strong evidence of system failure.

A valuable source of information about the impact of poor housing on the mental health of the community in general, and specifically on those already living with mental illness, is the final report of the Royal Commission into Victoria's Mental Health System, which was released in February 2021. The issue was important to the commission because social housing has been run down in Victoria more so than in other states and territories, and affordable housing is scarce. Many submissions were made to the commission declaring that the state's legacy of very low levels of social and affordable housing was both causing, and preventing people from recovering from, mental illness. The commission agreed with this assertion, as do I.

Poor housing and homelessness often interact with mental illness in a powerfully negative feedback loop. Those living with mental illness and psychological distress are more likely to have unsettled lives due to lack of affordable or social housing appropriate to their complex needs and, when necessary, to their care, treatment and support. They can often rotate through various kinds of accommodation, including private renting, boarding houses, couch surfing with family and friends, and emergency housing, and have periods of rough sleeping in-between or chronically. This worsens their mental ill-health and wellbeing, and harms their prospects of recovery.

Professor Karen Fisher of the Social Policy Research Centre at the University of New South Wales gave compelling expert evidence to the royal commission about this phenomenon:

The link between mental health and housing and homelessness is multi-directional—it is not just that housing affects mental health; mental health also affects housing. If someone has unstable housing then it is likely to extenuate the incidence and impact of pressures on their mental health by either causing mental ill health or causing other related conditions that affect mental health such as poverty, violence and disability. In the other direction, mental ill health without adequate support risks housing instability. The capacity of someone to maintain their housing, employment and social relations is affected by their mental health.[52]

These observations could equally be applied to the position of people with mental ill-health living in precarious housing anywhere in Australia. They also explain the intersecting and compounding impact of violation of both the right to housing and the right to mental health.

The fundamental importance of a home—in all the rich meaning of the term—to a person living with mental illness was compellingly demonstrated to me in my former judicial capacity by 'Patrick'.[53] He experienced an episode of acute mental illness for which he was compulsorily admitted as an inpatient to a secure mental hospital. Medical staff wanted to prevent him from returning to his modest home, which he continually tried to do, as they thought it was not in his best medical interests. They successfully obtained a guardianship order that would have resulted in his home being sold without his consent.

Patrick thought otherwise. He successfully challenged the order in court on legal and human rights grounds. The *Charter of Human Rights and Responsibilities Act*

2006 (Vic.) applied to the situation. It specifies the right to be free of arbitrary and unlawful interference with the home, which had not been properly considered. A man of a certain age, Patrick was eventually released from the secure ward to his home and commenced outpatient treatment. I have been told by colleagues in the consumer movement, where Patrick is 'a bit of a legend', that he recovered.

What would have happened to Patrick if he had not defended his human right to keep his home? To where would he have been discharged? Would he have been homeless? Would he have recovered or relapsed? What if he'd taken a private rental with the proceeds of the sale of his home, assuming he gained access to this money? Could he have managed the complexity of a private rental, and for how long would those proceeds have lasted? And what about social housing? Would he have been able to obtain and manage it? Or would he have become a casualty, if not a fatality, of the Australian housing disaster?

I think Patrick was a very good judge of his own best interests, and human rights provided protection of his exercise of that judgement when he needed it.

Housing and People Leaving Care

People living with disability or mental illness experience poor housing and homelessness more than the general population do, First People especially so. This may result in them being admitted to a medical or like facility. These circumstances are also associated with criminal offending, leading to imprisonment. From care or prison, they are too often discharged back to the very situation from which they came, including homelessness, where the wheel of social injustice may grind on. Commonwealth and state royal commissions and parliamentary inquiries have drawn attention to the problem.[54] It is a depressingly common experience of people working in the field to see this heartbreaking thing happen.

Certainly this is an aspect of the housing disaster, but it's also more than that. It is an aspect of the human rights disaster, one that involves governmental failure to ensure the right of people to a decent home, which has created conditions in which these poor life outcomes—outcomes that are inconsistent with a number of other human rights—occur in the first place, and then occur again.

Discharge into homelessness occurs in a number of different settings. Virtually all involve services operated by Commonwealth, state or territory government agencies who are bound to give effect to the right to a decent home, but do not. Government administration is siloed. If housing is another agency's responsibility but it does not make housing available, the discharge will often go ahead anyway. Too often this means homelessness for the person. This can and does happen in justice, health, mental health, disability support, aged care, rehabilitation and child-care settings.

From a humanitarian perspective, these situations are confronting, some extremely so. A large proportion of those discharged into homelessness are young people leaving state care at eighteen years of age. Some agencies discharge people to a motel for a night with a reference letter to a housing support agency, then leave them to fend for themselves. Prisoners might be discharged from the prison gate with a bus or train ticket and a food voucher. Where is the humanity in this? It is not rationally likely to achieve any sensible public policy outcome. It is certainly not consistent with Australia's human rights obligations.

Poor housing and the extreme risk of homelessness for discharged prisoners is a grave and worsening dimension of this general problem. For First People, it is an aspect of the cruel legacy of colonisation. And the prisoner population is growing, especially among Indigenous people. More than two in five (45 per cent) prison entrants report that they were homeless in the four weeks before prison (54 per cent for First People).[55] Prison entrants are 100 times more likely to be homeless than members of the general population (First People more so). The rise in prisoners is an aspect of the housing disaster, and it is placing the justice system under great strain.

Poor mental health and wellbeing, and poor or no housing, are two sides of the same coin. The prisoner population is likely to have had poor or no housing prior to, and poor mental health and wellbeing on, incarceration. Some 40 per cent of prisoners have mental health conditions, 33 per cent have cognitive disabilities, and 66 per cent have drug and alcohol misuse issues. These conditions are associated with precarious housing, offending and recidivism.[56] It is a notorious fact that prisoners do not get adequate medical treatment for mental ill-health in prison—I encountered the problem many times in my former judicial capacity. And yet prisoners are so often discharged back into the same circumstances. As Michael Mintrom has argued, this area would benefit from putting 'the progression of human rights at the heart of policymaking'.[57]

Human rights are not a privilege earnt by good behaviour. People imprisoned for offending lose their liberty for the period of the sentence, but they do not lose their human right to a decent home on release. Ensuring the right to a decent home of prisoners being released is a government human rights obligation. It is also crucial to desistance, reintegration, and providing support for those with complex needs, and can be very effective in breaking the imprisonment–homelessness cycle. I stress the importance of this in my capacity as a Victorian patron of the Justice Reform Initiative.[58]

It is very difficult for released prisoners to obtain private rentals because they face stigma and discrimination from landlords and prospective employers, and few affordable premises are available. There is strong evidence that public housing is the best option for released prisoners: former prisoners in public housing have markedly improved criminal justice outcomes. However, prisoner populations have risen at the same time that government support for public housing has fallen.[59] This makes the case for greater direct government investment in public housing all the stronger.

In these circumstances, it is unsurprising, but shocking nonetheless, that nearly half of prisoners (48 per cent) expect to be homeless on release. I cannot imagine what it must feel like to be in custody having that expectation. I am sure it is not pro-rehabilitation. No wonder recidivism rates are so high. This is another aspect of the housing disaster.

The late Uncle Jack Charles was the first person to give evidence to the Victorian Yoorrook Justice Commission on which I was serving. During a mid-morning break in proceedings in early 2021, I was standing with Uncle Jack outside Charcoal Lane in Gertrude Street, Fitzroy, where the hearing was being held. We were talking about his extraordinary life when a man in his early thirties walked past. He and Uncle Jack knew each other's mob. Uncle Jack greeted him warmly, introduced us, and asked him how he was going. The man said he had been released from prison that day and had just caught a train into the inner city. Uncle Jack asked where he was going, and the man said he had no idea; he asked him where he was going to live, and the man said he did not know. 'What about tonight,' said Uncle Jack, and the man shrugged his shoulders. Uncle Jack gave him an address of someone around the corner who might put him up. The man said he would go there. Uncle Jack then went back to the resumed hearing and gave historic evidence about the impact of colonisation on First People and how the justice system was a big part of the problem.

The man had been released from prison into homelessness. He went straight to Fitzroy, where First People have been going for decades because they feel at home there on Country with family and kin in a hostile world. There is always the possibility you will meet someone like Uncle Jack who might give you an ear and lend you a hand. That's what you need when government does not uphold your human rights, especially your right to a place to live when released from prison.

THE HUMAN RIGHT TO A DECENT HOME

Core Values

Values shape how the housing system is designed and operates with respect to people. The values of the private market, which have been dominant in the housing system for decades, see 'housing primarily as a commodity to be traded and as a vehicle for wealth creation'.[60] This has impeded the realisation of the human right to a decent home and contributed to the housing disaster. The values expressed by this right offer a different way of framing housing issues and reorienting the system.

Reflecting human rights generally, the values embodied by the right to a decent home are human-centred. Its core value is the equal and inherent dignity of all people. Its philosophical foundation is that persons are ends in themselves and not the means to others' ends. The purpose of this right is to ensure that all people have a decent home because this is indispensable for them to be able to live in dignity and develop in ways they personally choose with families and in society.

To be clear, a housing system based on the right to a decent home is not one where these human-centred values are simply noted, as they tend to be now. It is one where these values are brought into the system, whose operation is measured against them. Other values—like those underpinning the private market—may still have a role. As to the form of housing, human rights are tenure-neutral.[61] Human rights support home ownership as a form of housing that people may choose but not the only one. The human-centred purposes of the system are always paramount.

Colonisation and First People

Australian housing, one way or the other, is located on land taken from First People at colonisation, in what was a massive and systemic breach of their human rights. This is a fundamental truth of history. The foundations of Australia's market-based system of private land ownership were so established. The injustices of the original dispossession of land continue to impact First People today, while the benefits of that dispossession continue to accrue for the general population. As regards land and housing law and policy, this should be explicitly acknowledged and serious attention paid to its consequences.

For example, the right of First People to a decent home must be implemented in the light of the human right to equality. And it must be implemented substantively, which means more than equal access to housing for First People, for anything else would simply reinforce existing inequalities. It means positive measures to undo for them the continuing effects of past discrimination and exclusion in relation to land and housing arising from colonisation.

The right to a decent home is an inseparable part of the human rights framework under which First People have distinct economic, social, cultural and other rights, as specified in the *United Nations Declaration on the Rights of Indigenous Peoples* (UNDRIP), and founded upon the right to self-determination which it elaborates.

As recently recommended by the Commonwealth Parliament's Joint Standing Committee on Aboriginal and Torres Strait Islander Affairs, UNDRIP should be implemented by government as appropriate in law, policy and administration.[62] As regards First People, the right to a decent home must be interpreted and applied in a way that reflects UNDRIP and Indigenous people's history, culture and lived experiences. This has implications for how housing projects are carried out. They should be designed and led by First People based on their right to develop their own priorities and strategies. First People must also have the full opportunity to include land and housing in the voice, truth and treaty processes which are underway in Australia at some state and territory levels.

First People have a special relationship with land (and housing), which is part of their relationships with each other, both within and between their communities. They have a distinct world view in which land is spiritually central as a vital life force. A human rights–based approach to housing enables this special relationship and distinct world view to be reflected in the design and operation of the housing system.

International Law

In the absence of domestic law protecting and guaranteeing the right to a decent home, one can turn to international human rights law. Here, the right is to be found in the *International Bill of Rights*, which comprises the *United Nations Declaration on Human Rights*, the *International Covenant on Economic, Social and Cultural Rights* (ICESCR) and the *International Covenant on Civil and Political Rights* (ICCPR).

The housing component of the right is specified in the ICESCR as follows:

Article 11.1

The State Parties to the present Covenant recognize the right of everyone to an adequate standard of living for himself and his family, including adequate food, clothing and housing, and to the continuous improvement of living conditions …

The home component is specified in the ICCPR:

Article 17.1

No one shall be subjected to arbitrary or unlawful interference with his privacy, family, home or correspondence …

Australia is bound by international law to respect, protect and fulfil the right to a decent home because it is in the covenants, and it is also in a number of other international human rights treaties to which Australia is a party. The main argument of this book, which is that realising the right to a decent home should become the primary purpose of the housing system, could be done in a number of ways. Enshrining and implementing that purpose in Commonwealth and state and territory law would supply a strong foundation.

International law applies to countries with widely varying political, economic and social systems. It does not prescribe the kind of system to be adopted for human rights to be recognised and implemented. In relation to implementing the right to a decent home, the degree of reliance upon market and government mechanisms, and the mix between the two, is a matter for democratic choice in the state concerned, as long as the right is implemented equally for all. This necessarily involves consideration of the link between this right and other human rights, including the distinct rights of Indigenous people.

Similarly, states have divergent internal political, legal and administrative structures. Some have unitary systems, while others are federal in nature. Most states have local government of some kind. Responsibility for implementing human rights—including the right to a decent home—can be shared between different levels of government according to a national plan.

The Right to a Decent Home

The CESCR is the principal UN oversight authority for the ICESCR. One of its responsibilities is producing guidance on the meaning of the right to adequate housing in that covenant.[63] As that guidance makes clear, the right to housing is not to be interpreted in a narrow or restrictive way. It is a right to live somewhere in security, peace and dignity, and in the ICESCR it is linked with other human rights founded on the fundamental values of the covenant, which likewise reflect the inherent dignity of the human person. The scope of the right to housing encompasses the associated right in the ICCPR to be free of arbitrary or unlawful interference with the home.

The concept of 'adequacy' in the right to adequate housing is determined in part by social, economic, climatic, ecological and other factors that are country-specific. However, as stated by the CESCR, certain elements of the right must be considered in all contexts. These include what have been called the 'decency principles':

(a) legal security of tenure
(b) availability of services, materials, facilities and infrastructure
(c) affordability
(d) habitability
(e) accessibility
(f) location
(g) cultural adequacy.[64]

Principle (a) is implemented by laws and practices that protect different forms of tenure. It is clearly breached by weak residential tenancy laws in several Australian jurisdictions that allow forced eviction of tenants without cause, including tenants of public housing. I have previously expressed concern about this,[65] and I remain concerned about it. Principle (b) is supported by Australian laws that commonly specify minimum standards for all dwellings, including rented dwellings, private or public. Principle (c) is clearly breached in Australia because a feature of the housing disaster is widespread housing stress due to housing unaffordability. Principle (d) means that substandard housing is not permissible, while laws and regulations providing for minimum habitability standards are a means of implementing it. Principle (e) states a principle of accessibility for all as such. It is not only concerned with physical accessibility. Where affordable or social housing is scarce, it is not accessible. Housing in Australia poses significant accessibility challenges. Principle (f) applies in the Australian context, where a feature of the housing disaster is that people are being forced to buy or rent housing further and further away from employment, essential services, and family and social supports. Principle (g) is especially important in relation to First People.

Freedoms and Entitlements

The socially dominant conception of people in relation to housing is that the individual is personally responsible for it. If a person fails to find housing themselves, they may have to look to welfare programs administered by government, which may expand or contract as government chooses. If someone gets that assistance, too often they will be seen to be a personal failure—to be the passive recipient or beneficiary of that welfare.

The human rights conception of people in relation to housing is different. It sees all people as being in need of housing. Every person is an active rights-bearer who is empowered to make just claims on government for realisation of their rights, which cannot be rejected on purely policy grounds. People may achieve housing suitable for their needs in different ways, but government is responsible for establishing and maintaining a housing system whereby everyone can do so.

Rights-bearers can make claims under the human right to a decent home with respect to certain freedoms and entitlements. These freedoms and entitlements are reflected in the decency principles. An example of a freedom is the right to be free from arbitrary or unlawful eviction, as when the eviction is without cause, in retaliation against reasonable complaint, or done for discriminatory reasons. An example of an entitlement is the right to access emergency accommodation when needed, as when women and children need refuge from violence in their home.

Having the right to a decent home does not necessarily mean that rights-bearers get everything they want, when they want it, but it does mean their claim to a decent home when they need it can be made as a right. And as long as the rights-based order continues, it is not susceptible to rejection merely because of changes in government policy.

Duties and Obligations

For government as the duty-bearer, the human right to a decent home means that it must respect, protect and fulfil the freedoms and entitlements contained in the right. It must do so as a matter of obligation: one side of the right is the right of the person as the rights-bearer to the freedom or entitlement, and the other side is the obligation of government as the duty-bearer to uphold it. The obligation cannot be rejected as a matter of policy, unless of course government withdraws from the rights-based order itself. There is still significant scope for political contestation about housing issues, but this is about how, and not whether, the right should be implemented. Government has a certain 'margin of discretion' about how best to implement the right. Managing scarce resources (even in wealthy countries like Australia) and determining priorities and making trade-offs are an inevitable part of doing so. Also, having this duty does not mean that government must act to realise everyone's access to housing immediately and fully. But it does mean that the primary function of the system is to realise the right.

Progressive Realisation

As just described, the right to a decent home gives rise to freedoms and entitlements for people as rights-bearers, and duties and obligations for government as the duty bearer. But people are not entitled to insist on their rights being realised immediately (although there are certain minima). Full implementation of those aspects of the right which involve the allocation of scarce public resources can be progressively realised over time given the availability of those resources and other reasonable constraints.

However, governments cannot use the principle of progressive realisation as a back-door way of avoiding their human rights obligations. Government must always take steps that are 'deliberate, concrete and targeted as clearly as possible' towards the realisation of the right, and it must 'move as expeditiously and effectively as possible' towards full realisation of the right.[66]

Core Obligations

While the right to a decent home can be progressively realised, there are 'minimum core obligations' that must be realised immediately. For example, government must refrain from direct discrimination against people for prohibited reasons, such as disability, sex or race. Also, it has an obligation to provide 'basic shelter and housing' to people who need it, which includes the obligation to provide temporary emergency housing when needed. This means significant homelessness, as exists in Australia, is a violation of the right to adequate housing in respect of the minimum core obligation. Finally, government has a core obligation of immediate effect to provide emergency housing to women and children fleeing violence in their homes.[67]

Obligation to Respect, Protect and Fulfil

The United Nations has endorsed and applied principles in relation to different kinds of obligations that government has when applying human rights, whatever the nature of the right, and including the right to a decent home.[68] These principles help in understanding what must be done to give effect to rights, in making claims for rights to be upheld, and in designing accountability and governance mechanisms as part of a human rights framework or plan. They are supported by a significant body of scholarship.[69]

To give a summary, there are three elements to the obligation of government to give effect to human rights: to respect, protect and fulfil the right.

1   *The obligation to respect the right.* This obligation places a responsibility on government to refrain from interfering directly or indirectly with the enjoyment

of a right by all persons. For example, government must not discriminate in the provision of public housing, forcibly evict tenants from public housing without reason or procedural fairness, provide public housing that is unsafe, or charge unaffordable rent for public housing.

2 *The obligation to protect the right.* This obligation places a responsibility on government to prevent third parties from interfering with the enjoyment of the right by all persons. For example, government must take reasonable steps to ensure that private landlords do not discriminate in the provision of rental housing, provide substandard housing, or evict tenants without cause. This obligation imposes on government a responsibility to put in place a legislative and administrative framework that guarantees these aspects of the right to a decent home. In most jurisdictions in Australia, no such framework has been put in place to guarantee the right to security of tenure and give protection from eviction without cause.

3 *The obligation to fulfil the right.* This obligation requires government to take all necessary and appropriate measures to ensure the full realisation of the right by all persons, including legislative, administrative and public finance measures. For example, government must create a housing system that enables all people to have access to a decent home, taking into

account the decency principles. This will require a legislative framework, departments of state, public finance and intergovernmental arrangements that reflect divisions of responsibility within the political system in the country concerned. The causes of the housing disaster in Australia involve many failures by government to fulfil the right to a decent home.

Having regard to rights and obligations of the human right to a decent home as explained here, I now want to explore how these may be used to reorient the housing system.

REORIENTING THE HOUSING SYSTEM

A Human Rights–Based Strategy

The housing system in Australia has four components— home ownership, private rental housing, social housing and homelessness—in which every level of government plays some role. It is large and complex. Addressing the housing disaster requires a coordinated response across all of those parts of the system and levels of government. It requires an effective strategy covering legislation, policy development and coordination, tax and finance, building and construction, labour availability, planning and other aspects. It needs to be whole-of-government and inter-governmental and, I contend, human rights–based.

A major cause of the housing disaster is that the system has no overarching strategy of this kind, human rights–based or otherwise. The Productivity Commission drew attention to this in its review of the National Housing and Homelessness Agreement, which it described as 'a funding contract, not a blueprint for reform'.[70] This correctly implies that a blueprint for reform is needed. The commission emphasised the importance of 'housing first'-type approaches to ending homelessness (which are based on human rights), saying they should be scaled up.

The lack of such a strategy has been a longstanding issue. In 2006, Miloon Kathari, the then UN special rapporteur on the right to adequate housing, visited Australia. Kathari reported that there was a 'serious national housing crisis in Australia' and that there was 'no national legislative or policy framework' in place, recommending that:

> Australia should adopt a comprehensive and coordinated national housing policy, and develop a clear, consistent, long-term and holistic housing strategy that addresses structural problems, is efficient, and embodies an overarching human rights approach, with the primary task of meeting the needs of the most vulnerable groups.[71]

This recommendation is still relevant today. Things have only gotten worse since then.

There is not one definition of 'an overarching human rights approach', but one could easily be developed to meet Australian conditions. Leilani Fahra has given guidance on how this could be done with regard to housing systems. She defined the approach as being based on ten principles:

1   based in law and legal standards
2   prioritise those most in need and ensure equality
3   comprehensive and whole of government
4   rights-based participation
5   accountable budgeting and tax justice
6   human rights–based goals and timelines
7   accountability and monitoring
8   ensure access to justice
9   clarify the obligations of private actors and regulating financial, housing and real estate markets
10 implement international cooperation and assistance.[72]

The Australian Human Rights Commission's general definition is similar.[73]

Several comparable countries have adopted a human rights approach to designing and implementing affordable housing and homelessness strategies. One example is Canada. Like Australia, it is a former British colony with a substantial indigenous population still experiencing ongoing injustices, and it has similar housing problems to Australia's, with similar causes.

Previous policy-based approaches have failed, as they have here, so Canada has decided to innovate. It has taken a human rights turn, as I suggest Australia should. The result, in 2019, was the enactment by the federal parliament of the *National Housing Strategy Act*, which declared that the housing policy of Canada recognised the right to adequate housing and that government was obligated to realise this right for all. It stated that the minister for housing must 'develop and maintain a national housing strategy to further the housing policy, taking into account key principles of a human rights-based approach to housing'.[74] The Act also established a number of institutions to facilitate the process, including a National Housing Council.

Canada has developed and implemented strategies under the Act, but it is still early days. The council has assisted the government to design and enact the strategies. It has emphasised the magnitude of the task and the importance of national leadership if the right to adequate housing is to be realised.[75] This is surely true for Australia as well. The most recent Canadian strategy, released in April 2024, is the most comprehensive so far, impressive in its scope and ambition.[76]

In Australia, attention has rightly turned to the potential for this approach to be adopted. Chris Martin and his colleagues at AHURI produced a major report on the subject in 2023 that reviewed international best practice, including the Canadian innovation. Its main recommendation was that 'Australia should have a Housing and Homelessness Strategy with a mission: everyone in Australia has adequate housing'.[77] I agree, and it should follow a human rights–based approach, consistent with this mission.

Australia commenced the development of a National Housing and Homelessness Plan in 2023, which is very welcome. An issues paper has been released, a process of consultation was opened and is now closed, and the matter is under consideration. The issues paper is comprehensive (except that, notably, it does not include taxation policy) and demonstrates the federal government's desire for national leadership. But it is policy-based, and neither rights-based nor legislation-based. By contrast, many of the consultation responses spoke of need for the national plan to be rights-based.[78]

If the plan remains purely policy-based and does not have legislative backing, as seems to be the present intention, I fear that it will not succeed in overcoming Australia's housing disaster nor prevent it from reoccurring. The situation is so serious that we should aim to do something that is transformative and ambitious, and I am not sure this will be.

Values produce actions and outcomes. If you do not have the right values, you will not have the right actions and outcomes. Valuing housing primarily as a commodity for private investment is deeply entrenched in the system. It is a structural cause of the housing disaster which must be addressed. The values underlying the system will not be changed by purely policy-based, non-legislative approaches.

For this change to happen, Australia needs to legislate a different enabling environment for the housing system. It must be explicitly based on realising the human right to a decent home—and be linked with the enactment of comprehensive human rights legislation at the federal, state and territory levels. This is a necessary part of the structural change that the system needs. The plan should be backed by legislation as a fully worked out strategy for ending, not just ameliorating, the housing disaster. It should be directed at meeting, over time, the actual needs—legacy, present and future—of people with respect to affordable housing, social housing and homelessness, not just improving on present and past national efforts. It should follow the principles of the human rights–based approach as adapted to Australian conditions.

Comprehensive Human Rights Legislation

Australia is not one of the dozens of countries that have a constitutional right to housing. It does not yet have a national human rights Act. We are the only liberal democracy without comprehensive legal human rights protection in our Constitution or such an Act. This is long overdue and rightly under serious consideration.[79]

Australia does not legally guarantee access to emergency housing for those living with homelessness, as in the United Kingdom. Nor is Australia part of a regional human rights treaty framework that specifies the right to a decent home, as in Europe.

Australia does have some legislative human rights protection. For example, Queensland, Victoria and the Australian Capital Territory have human rights Acts that specify the right to be free of arbitrary and unlawful interference with the home. The case of 'Patrick' in Victoria shows how powerful this right can be in protecting the home. Even so, the human rights obligations of governments under these Acts are not yet strongly enforceable, do not include the right to adequate housing, and do not constitute a general right to a decent home. Jessie Hohmann has shown how international, European and South African precedents could inform the inclusion of the right to housing in state and territory human rights Acts.[80]

Another example is that, when Commonwealth legislation is proposed, a parliamentary committee must scrutinise the proposed Bill to see if it complies with international human rights, including the right to a decent home.[81] The state and territory human rights Acts establish similar pre-legislative scrutiny mechanisms.

A final example is that access to housing as a service is protected by Commonwealth, state and territory anti-discrimination, disability and like legislation.

However, the patchwork quilt of domestic human rights protection in Australia has more holes than patches, and it does not recognise or guarantee the right to a decent home. The housing disaster is proof positive that comprehensive human rights protection is desperately needed and should include the right to a decent home. The lack of this protection in Australia has allowed a skewed enabling environment in the housing system to thrive—one where housing is seen primarily as a commodity to be used for wealth creation rather than a home. This needs to change.

Comprehensive human rights protection is a necessary part of creating this change. The housing system is part of a wider system of government with which it interacts in all sorts of ways. Bringing all human rights into government as a whole will make the right to a decent home stronger in the housing system. There should be comprehensive human rights Acts at the national, state and territory levels that cover economic, social and cultural rights, including the right to a decent home, as well as civil and political rights. They should bind government, and all non-government agencies who provide social housing, including community housing. They should work alongside and in support of the national legislative rights-based housing strategy in creating a new enabling environment that is supportive of the primary value of housing as a home for people.

Reforming Residential Tenancies Legislation

As I have argued elsewhere,[82] the values behind the common law regulation of rental housing are freedom of contract and property rights. Rental housing is not a field of law in itself. It should be, one based on human rights values, but that will only come with legislation we don't yet have.

The common law is basically the same whether the premises are being rented for a home or a business, or by a person or a corporation. The parties are conceived as having the capacity freely to enter into a contract of tenancy on the agreed terms, from which the tenant obtains exclusive possession of the premises and the landlord obtains the rent, while retaining the right of ownership. Inequality of bargaining power is ignored for virtually all purposes.

Under the common law, where the contract is written, the length of the tenancy is as specified. At the end, the tenant can be evicted without any more cause than the end of the tenancy. If a new written tenancy is agreed to, the process starts again. If the tenant is simply allowed to stay on without another agreement, the tenancy becomes periodic, say month to month, and the tenant can be evicted on a month's notice. Where a tenancy is oral and not in writing, the tenancy will automatically become periodic and it is the same. The landlord does not have to give reasons for doing anything, like evicting the tenant, because the property is theirs to do with as they like. The purpose of the law is mainly to protect the owner's property rights. Where the place is the tenant's home, this doesn't come into it. It doesn't matter that they have lived there for years, or that they might be homeless on eviction. Such is the way of the common law.

My first case as an advocate in the Supreme Court of Victoria was in 1978. It was a scary experience. I had completed arts/law at Monash University, had just been admitted and was working at the Tenants' Union. An older woman living with mental illness was being evicted from a periodic tenancy and she was traumatised. The landlord, who I believe just wanted to get rid of the woman, didn't have to give a reason for giving her four weeks' notice to vacate. Fortunately for the woman, the landlord made a technical error in the notice—it should have been a month's notice, not four weeks. That was enough before a sympathetic judge to get a temporary injunction against the eviction, which slowed it down a bit. But only a bit. The woman was eventually forced to leave her home, without cause. Again, such is the way of the common law.

Extraordinarily, without special legislation, it is the same with social housing, because the legal relationship is also that of landlord and tenant. In the postwar period, hundreds of thousands of Australian families, including the one in which I grew up, lived in public rental housing as tenants of the government landlord without any security of tenure. Nobody knew until there was reason to, but as renters under a periodic tenancy we were utterly at the system's mercy. The housing commissions developed bad reputations for paternalism and authoritarianism, and First People's stories about this can be quite horrific. This is one reason why Menzies' policy of allowing sitting public tenants to buy their homes was so successful. It meant they could escape the housing commissions. In some Australian jurisdictions it is better with social housing these days, but still not fully secure.

A feeling of insecurity about rental housing, including public rental housing, is embedded in Australian culture. It is a product of historically weak tenancy laws only partly reformed in the modern era. It is one reason why rental housing is seen to be second-best. Rental housing needs to be rehabilitated as a form of tenure. It won't be easy, but taking human rights seriously in regulating rental housing will help.

The *International Covenant on Economic, Social and Cultural Rights* came into force in 1976. It wasn't long before word got around among grassroots activists in Australia that it included a right to housing. Beginning with Victoria in the late 1970s, campaigns began for tenancy law reform across Australia. I want to pay tribute to Mike Salvaris for his leadership of the Victorian campaign. Unfortunately, the right to housing became just a background consideration, like it is in the housing system now. Australia didn't understand the relevance of the international human right to a decent home, and this is hardly surprising. Other more familiar but less demanding ways of making the case for long overdue reform were promoted: social justice, abuse of power by landlords, estate agents keeping bond money, reducing poverty and so on. The work of the Australian Government Commission of Inquiry into Poverty helped in this endeavour.[83]

In consequence, in the 1980s and thereafter, legislation was passed in the states and territories that provided a degree of welcome protection for tenants and established tenancy tribunals. But it was very soft-touch reform. Eviction without cause was not abolished. The new tenancy tribunals were required to process the masses of eviction applications, but in a humane way. Full human rights–based reform did not occur but rather became unfinished business, and remains so.

I reviewed the legislation in all the states and territories in 2012 against human rights standards, and specifically as regards security of tenure.[84] I found that most of the residential tenancy legislation at that time did not provide security of tenure for tenants, even social housing tenants. They permitted eviction without cause, and most still do. There has been movement in the right direction in some jurisdictions, especially in Victoria, but not far or quickly enough.

The weakness of residential tenancy regulation in Australia is a feature of the housing disaster for two reasons. It has resulted in insecure tenure for nearly one-third of Australian households, and it has contributed to the second-best reputation that rental housing has in Australia as a form of tenure. This has placed unnecessary strain on the housing system as a whole, and still does.

In 2023, National Cabinet agreed to 'harmonise and strengthen renters' rights across Australia' in three ways: a nationally consistent approach requiring reasonable grounds for eviction; moving towards limiting rent increases to once a year; and phasing in minimum rental standards.[85] This is a very welcome and urgent task, but I suggest that the reforms need to be more explicitly linked to, and implement, human rights standards.

Residential tenancy legislation in the states and territories should be reformed in line with the decency principles, especially legal security of tenure; availability of services, materials, facilities and infrastructure; and habitability. A measure of rent regulation is needed to implement the principle of affordability. The reformed legislation should apply to all rental housing, both private and social—and with social housing, it should apply to both government and community rental housing. General human rights obligations in state and territory human rights Acts must apply to both government and community providers of rental social housing as part of a general package of human rights protection for this form of housing.

CONCLUSION

Australia is experiencing a disaster in all parts of its housing system. Home ownership is so unaffordable as to be out of reach for increasingly large numbers of people, even households with two average wages coming in. Renting is the only option for many, but this too is more unaffordable—and scarcer—than ever, and tenancy regulation is not fit for modern purpose in most jurisdictions. Social housing is very difficult to obtain because what little there is goes to those in greatest need after waiting up to a decade or more. With housing being so hard to access, is it any wonder that homelessness is so high? Stories are regularly publicised about women sleeping in cars that shock the public conscience. Certain groups, including First People, are affected even more grievously than others.

Unfortunately, that paragraph could have been written ten or even twenty years ago and been accurate without changing a word. Many people besides myself have drawn attention to this problem without it being resolved—indeed, with it only getting worse. The way we are going, the same paragraph may be written ten or twenty years hence with equal accuracy.

What a deeply troubling prospect. If this happens, the housing crisis will have existed for three to four decades. And what then? We are not going to make the SDG target of ensuring 'access to all to adequate, safe and affordable housing' by 2030 despite being one of the wealthiest countries on earth. How can we expect other countries to develop sustainably when we are not doing so ourselves?

The situation we confront has been oft-called a crisis. Maybe that was a fair enough description a generation ago. But now it is obviously not just a blip in an otherwise well-functioning system. It is chronic. It has become the system. That is why we need a stronger word to describe what is unfolding. I have chosen the word 'disaster', but if it continues for much longer, it will be a catastrophe. And this terrible evolution will have been absolutely predictable and avoidable, all on our moral watch.

There is still time to act, however. Successive Australian governments have framed housing the population purely as a matter of socioeconomic policy, except that it is now the other way around. The economic value of housing as an investment has been allowed to dominate the social value of housing as a home. That is a skewed way of looking at a fundamental human need that is embodied in a fundamental human right. Yet it has come to define the entire housing system. That is the root cause of our dilemma. That way of looking at housing has to change.

National funding for different kinds of housing, including funding by way of taxation expenditures, has varied since World War II. In the postwar period, direct government funding of housing increased, then fell off. Never have direct funding and other necessary measures been sustained for long enough, or been sufficient, to meet the level of proven need for affordable and social housing, and to end homelessness. Especially since 2000, massive taxation expenditures supporting home ownership have contributed to the disaster. In the contemporary era, direct national funding for housing has been rising from a very low base. But the purpose of these increases is to lift the funding effort, not meet the forecast need, which remains high. Where will this leave us in the next decade or two?

Past approaches to framing housing issues have failed and they must change. We need to make the realisation of housing as the 'Great Australian Right' the purpose of the system, and achieving this purpose must be government's primary responsibility. There will still be wide scope for socioeconomic policy to be democratically debated, developed and implemented, but consistently with the human right to a decent home.

For this to occur, there must be a national housing and homelessness plan that is rights-based, comprehensive, strategic and legislated.

To be rights-based, it must have the purpose of realising the right to a decent home for all and apply human rights–based principles in doing so. This means balanced support for all potential forms of tenure, taking into account the decency principles. In relation to First People, it means the plan must be linked to and consistent with the *Universal Declaration on the Rights of Indigenous Peoples.*

To be comprehensive, it must cover all parts of the system, because they are interdependent. Among other things, this means state and territory residential tenancies legislation must be reformed in line with human rights, especially the right to a decent home. In particular, it means the scourge of eviction without just cause must finally and categorically be ended in all jurisdictions.

To be strategic, it must specify ways and means for ensuring over time the right to a decent home for all and the end to homelessness, not just lifting the funding effort, important as this is.

Finally, to be legislated, the plan must be supported by legislation that is strong enough to achieve its historic purpose, drawing on overseas experience. Because it will support human rights in the housing system and across the whole of government, a national human rights Act should also be legislated, including the right to a decent home and other economic, social and cultural rights, as recently recommended by the Commonwealth Parliamentary Joint Committee on Human Rights.

NOTES

1   Unless otherwise stated, the statistics quoted in this section come from: National Housing Supply and Affordability Council (NHSAC), *State of the Housing System 2024*, Commonwealth of Australia, 2024, pp. 8, 11, 34, 44, 62, 73, 82, 88, 95, 100, 105, 115, 118; and Productivity Commission, *In Need of Repair: The National Housing and Homelessness Agreement*, Commonwealth of Australia, August 2022, pp. 6, 18, 204, 232, 245, 263, 296, 348, 350, 353.

2   United Nations, 'Resolution adopted by the General Assembly on 25 September 2015', doc. A/RES/70/1, 25 September 2015.

3   United Nations, *International Covenant on Economic, Social and Cultural Rights*, 1966, article 11.1; and United Nations, *International Covenants on Civil and Political Rights*, 1966, article 17.1. See also United Nations, *Universal Declaration of Human Rights*, 1948, articles 12 and 25.1.

4   Productivity Commission, *In Need of Repair*, p. 348.

5   Alan Kohler, 'The Great Divide', *Quarterly Essay*, no. 92, November 2023, p. 6.

6 Productivity Commission, *In Need of Repair*, p. 353.

7 NHSAC, *State of the Housing System 2024*, p. 95.

8 Chris Martin et al., *Towards an Australian Housing and Homelessness Strategy: Understanding National Approaches in Contemporary Policy*, Final Report No. 401, Australian Housing and Urban Research Institute, 15 June 2013, p. 12.

9 NHSAC, *State of the Housing System 2024*, p. 108.

10 SQM Research, 'Vacancy Rates Remained Steady at 1.0%', press release, 16 April 2024.

11 Martin et al., *Towards an Australian Housing and Homelessness Strategy*, p. 12.

12 Courtney Withers, 'Rental Affordability in Australia Is as Bad as It Has Ever Been, According to New Anglicare Australia Report', *ABC News*, 23 April 2024.

13 Productivity Commission, *In Need of Repair*, p. 296.

14 Brendan Coates, 'The Great Australian Nightmare', 131st Annual Henry George Commemorative Lecture, Grattan Institute, Melbourne, 14 September 2022, part 4.

15 Productivity Commission, *In Need of Repair*, p. 263.

16 NHSAC, *State of the Housing System 2024*, p. 34.

17 Productivity Commission, *In Need of Repair*, p. 245.

18 Rachel Ong ViforJ, 'Our Housing System Is Broken and the Poorest Australians Are Being Hardest Hit', *The Conversation*, 24 April 2024.

19 Martin et al., *Towards an Australian Housing and Homelessness Strategy*, pp. 13–14; NHSAC, *State of the Housing System 2024*, p. 115.

20 Australian Bureau of Statistics (ABS), 'Census of Population and Housing: Census Dictionary', 2021. The Australian human rights housing scholar Jessie Hohmann refers to the privacy, identity and space dimensions of

housing in *The Right to Housing: Law, Concepts and Possibilities*, Hart Publishing, 2013, chs 6, 7 and 8.

21 ABS, 'Estimating Homelessness: Census', 2021.

22 Ibid.

23 ABS, 'General Social Survey: Summary Results, Australia', 2019.

24 Productivity Commission, *In Need of Repair*, p. 307 (anonymised case study from a case worker in western Melbourne provided by Tenants Victoria).

25 Martin et al., *Towards an Australian Housing and Homelessness Strategy*, p. 14, citing Productivity Commission, *In Need of Repair*, p. 204.

26 United Nations, *Guidelines for the Implementation of the Right to Adequate Housing*, report of the special rapporteur on adequate housing, doc. A/HRC/43/43, 25 December 2019, para. 30.

27 'Mr J. T. Gellibrand's Memoranda of a Trip to Port Phillip in 1836', *Transactions of the Philosophical Institute of Victoria*, vol. 3, 1859, p. 69.

28 See, generally, AW Howitt, *The Native Tribes of South-East Victoria*, Aboriginal Studies Press, 1996; Robert Brough Smyth, *Aborigines of Victoria*, Cambridge University Press, facsimile edn, 2010, vols 1 and 2.

29 Jessie Hohmann, 'Toward a Right to Housing for Australia: Reframing Affordability Debates through Article 11(1) of the *International Covenant on Economic, Social and Cultural Rights*', *Australian Journal of Human Rights*, vol. 1, 2020, p. 11.

30 Kohler, 'The Great Divide', pp. 25–8; Peter Mares, *No Place Like Home: Repairing Australia's Housing Crisis*, Text Publishing 2018, p. 268.

31 For example, in Victoria, the voice is the First Peoples'
    Assembly of Victoria, the truth process is the Yoorrook
    Justice Commission (on which I served), and the treaty
    making-process is constituted by the elements of the
    Victorian Treaty Framework. For Queensland, see
    the *Path to Treaty Act 2023*, and for South Australia,
    see the *First Nations Voice Act 2023*. Similar processes
    are being considered in other states.

32 See the United Nations, *United Nations Declaration on the
    Rights of Indigenous Peoples*, 2007.

33 Commonwealth Housing Commission, *Final Report*,
    Ministry of Post-War Reconstruction, 25 August 1944,
    letter of transmission (emphasis in original).

34 Patrick Troy, 'The Commonwealth Housing Commission
    and National Housing Policy', paper, fourth State
    of Australian Cities National Conference, Perth,
    27 November 2009.

35 See especially Jim Kemeny, *The Great Australian
    Nightmare*, Georgian House, 1983, ch. 1.

36 Judith Brett, 'Correspondence', *Quarterly Essay*, no. 93,
    March 2024, p. 131.

37 Mares, *No Place Like Home*, p. 272.

38 NHSAC, *State of the Housing System 2024*, esp. chs 2, 3
    and 8.

39 Kohler, 'The Great Divide'; Saul Eslake, '50 Years of Policy
    Failure', 122nd Annual Henry George Commemorative
    Lecture, 2 September 2013; Coates, 'The Great Australian
    Nightmare'; Productivity Commission, *In Need of
    Repair*; Martin et al., *Towards an Australian Housing and
    Homelessness Strategy*.

40 Kohler, 'The Great Divide', pp. 7, 9.

41 NHSAC, *State of the Housing System 2024*, p. 7.

42 National Housing Finance and Investment Corporation, *State of the Nation's Housing 2022–23*, 2023, p. 101.

43 Productivity Commission, *In Need of Repair*, p. 263.

44 Ryan van den Nouwelant, Laurence Troy and Balamurugan Soundararaj, 'Quantifying Australia's Unmet Housing Need: A National Snapshot', Community Housing Industry Association, November 2022.

45 See Columbia Law School, 'Kimberlé Crenshaw on Intersectionality, More than Two Decades Later'.

46 Australian Institute of Health and Welfare (AIHW), 'The Health of People in Australia's Prisons 2022', 15 November 2023.

47 Christopher Knaus and Nick Evershed, 'What Do We Know about Homelessness Deaths in Australia— and Why Is Nobody Tracking Them?', *The Guardian*, 6 February 2024.

48 United Nations, 'Adequate Housing as a Component of the Right to an Adequate Standard of Living', doc. A/71/310, 8 August 2016, para. 27.

49 United Nations, *General Comment No. 36 on Article 6: Right to Life*, doc. CCPR/C/GC/36, 3 September 2019, para. 30.

50 See Richard Broome, 'They Had Little Chance', *Historical Journal*, vol. 91, no. 2, 2020, p. 245.

51 United Nations, *General Comment No. 14: The Right to the Highest Attainable Standard of Health*, doc. E/C.12/2004/4, 11 August 2000, para. 3.

52 Royal Commission into Victoria's Mental Health System, *Final Report*, vol. 2, February 2021, p. 403.

53 *PJB v Melbourne Health (Patrick's Case)* (2011) 39 VR 373 (Bell J); [2011] VSC 327 (31 January 2011).

54 Royal Commission into Violence, Abuse, Neglect and Exploitation of People with Disability, *Final Report*, vol. 7: *Inclusive Education, Employment and Housing*, 2023, part C, pp. 589–90 (see also Productivity Commission, *In Need of Repair*, p. 25); Legislative Council, Legal and Social Issues Committee, *Inquiry into Homelessness, Final Report*, Parliament of Victoria, 2021, p. 174.

55 AIHW, 'The Health of People in Australia's Prisons 2022'.

56 Martin et al., *Towards an Australian Housing and Homelessness Strategy*, p. 24.

57 Michael Mintrom, *Advancing Human Rights*, Monash University Publishing, 2022, p. 15.

58 The Justice Reform Initiative is an alliance of Australians committed to reforming the criminal justice system.

59 The AIHW provided information on clients exiting custodial arrangements in its *Specialist Homelessness Services Annual Report 2022–23*, 2024. Also see Martin et al., *Towards an Australian Housing and Homelessness Strategy*, pp. 24, 33, 53.

60 Russell Solomon, *Australia's Engagement with Economic and Social Rights: A Case of Institutional Avoidance*, Palgrave Macmillan, 2021, p. 255.

61 See Nico Moons, *The Right to Housing in Law and Society*, Routledge, 2018, p. 58.

62 See Wayne Atkinson and Kevin Bell, 'Following the Voice Failure, Indigenous Politicians Are Calling for the UN's Declaration on the Rights of Indigenous Peoples to Be Implemented. What Is It and What Would It Mean?', *The Conversation*, 15 January 2024.

63 United Nations, *General Comment No. 4: The Right to Adequate Housing*, doc. E/1992/23, 13 December 1991.

64 Te Kāhui Tika Tangata / New Zealand Human Rights Commission, *Framework Guidelines on the Right to a Decent Home in Aotearoa*, 2021, p. 25. This report has informed the structure and content of this section.

65 Kevin Bell, 'Protecting Public Housing Tenants in Australia from Forced Eviction: The Fundamental Importance of the Human Right to Adequate Housing and Home', *Monash University Law Review*, vol. 39, 2012, p. 1. Reforms have since occurred in Victoria, the ACT and Queensland.

66 United Nations, *General Comment No. 3: The Nature of State Parties' Obligations*, doc. E/199/23, 14 December 1990, paras 9–12.

67 Ibid., para 10.

68 United Nations, *The Maastricht Guidelines on Violations of Economic, Social and Cultural Rights*, doc. E/C.12/2000/13, 2 October 2000.

69 The tripartite obligation schema was expounded by Asbjorn Eide, the UN special rapporteur on the right to adequate food. See United Nations, *Report on the Right to Adequate Food as a Human Right*, doc. E/CN.4/Sub.2/1987/23, 7 July 1987.

70 Productivity Commission, *In Need of Repair*, p. 2.

71 United Nations, *Report of the Special Rapporteur on Adequate Housing as a Component of the Right to an Adequate Standard of Living*, doc. A/HRC/4/18/Add.2, 11 May 2007, p. 2 and para. 127.

72 United Nations, *Report of the Special Rapporteur on Adequate Housing as a Component of the Right to an*

Adequate Standard of Living, note by the secretariat, doc. A/HRC/37/53, 15 January 2018.

73 Australian Human Rights Commission, 'Our Approach', 2024.

74 *National Housing Strategy Act 2019* (Can), sections 4, 5(1).

75 National Housing Council, *The Right to Adequate Housing: What It Means and Why It Matters for Addressing Canada's Housing Affordability Crisis*, 2024.

76 Infrastructure Canada, *Solving the Housing Crisis: Canada's Housing Plan*, Canadian Government, 2024.

77 Martin et al., *Towards an Australian Housing and Homelessness Strategy*, p. 1.

78 Department of Social Services, 'Developing the National Housing and Homelessness Plan', Commonwealth of Australia, 2024. See the issues paper, consultation summary report and submissions.

79 See Australian Human Rights Commission, 'A Human Rights Act for Australia', 2022. Beginning in 2023, at the request of the attorney-general, the Commonwealth Parliamentary Joint Committee on Human Rights conducted an inquiry into the adequacy of Australia's human rights protections, including whether a human rights Act should be enacted. The report has been released: see *Inquiry into Australia's Human Rights Framework, Report—May 2024*. It recommends that a comprehensive human rights Act be legislated containing the civil and political rights, and the economic, social and cultural rights, including the rights to home and housing.

80 Jessie Hohmann, 'A Right to Housing for the Victorian *Charter of Human Rights and Responsibilities*? Assessing Potential Models under the *International Covenant on*

Economic, Social and Cultural Rights; the *European Social Charter*; and the *South African Constitution*', *Monash Law Review*, vol. 48, no. 2, 2022, p. 133.

81 *Human Rights (Parliamentary Scrutiny) Act 2011* (Cth).

82 Kevin Bell, 'Protecting Public Housing Tenants', pp. 5–6.

83 See Adrian Bradbrook, *Poverty and the Landlord–Tenant Relationship*, Australian Government Publishing Service, 1975.

84 Bell, 'Protecting Public Housing Tenants'.

85 Anthony Albanese, 'Meeting of National Cabinet', press release, 16 August 2023, attachment 2: 'A Better Deal for Renters'.

(continued from previous page)

Andrew Jaspan & Lachlan Guselli *The Consultancy Conundrum: The Hollowing Out of the Public Sector*

Andrew Leigh *Fair Game: Lessons from Sport for a Fairer Society & a Stronger Economy*

Ian Lowe *Australia on the Brink: Avoiding Environmental Ruin*

John Lyons *Dateline Jerusalem: Journalism's Toughest Assignment*

Richard Marles *Tides that Bind: Australia in the Pacific*

Fiona McLeod *Easy Lies & Influence*

Michael Mintrom *Advancing Human Rights*

Louise Newman *Rape Culture*

Martin Parkinson *A Decade of Drift*

Jennifer Rayner *Climate Clangers: The Bad Ideas Blocking Real Action*

Isabelle Reinecke *Courting Power: Law, Democracy & the Public Interest in Australia*

Abul Rizvi *Population Shock*

Kevin Rudd *The Case for Courage*

Don Russell *Leadership*

Scott Ryan *Challenging Politics*

Ronli Sifris *Towards Reproductive Justice*

Kate Thwaites & Jenny Macklin *Enough Is Enough*

Simon Wilkie *The Digital Revolution: A Survival Guide*

Carla Wilshire *Time to Reboot: Feminism in the Algorithm Age*

Campbell Wilson *Living with AI*